CW00732630

GEORGE & ROBERT STEPHENSON

To Jenny, Vicky and Ross

GEORGE & ROBERT STEPHENSON

How *Rocket* Science Reshaped the World

ROBIN JONES

First published in Great Britain in 2011

British Library Cataloguing-in-Publication Data
A CIP record for this title is available from the British Library

ISBN 978 0 85710 057 3

PiXZ Books
Halsgrove House, Ryelands Business Park,
Bagley Road, Wellington, Somerset TA21 9PZ
Tel: 01823 653777
Fax: 01823 216796
email: sales@halsgrove.com

An imprint of Halstar Ltd, part of the Halsgrove group of companies
Information on all Halsgrove titles is available at: www.halsgrove.com

Printed and bound in China by Toppan Leefung Printing Ltd

In the autumn of 2010, Steve Davies, director of Britain's multiple-award-winning National Railway Museum in York, unveiled a £21-million blueprint for a major redesign of the venue, in order to ensure that its outstanding contribution to heritage and education will be retained for future generations, all of whom will have no first-hand recollection of steam in regular service on the country's national railway network.

The centrepiece of the redesign is a bridge link connecting a new visitor entrance to the Great Hall, a former steam locomotive roundhouse shed. The bridge has been designed to offer a grandstand view of the exhibits below, all of which will reflect landmarks in two centuries of railway evolution.

However, one locomotive exhibit has been pencilled in to be positioned on the bridge itself, to greet the millions of visitors, as a, or rather the, definitive introduction to the subject. It is the museum's static replica of Stephenson's *Rocket*, the locomotive that mapped out the course of global transport history.

Left: *George Stephenson.*

*An artist's impression of the static replica of Rocket on the bridge
inside the revamped National Railway Museum at York.*

Most if not all visitors of the museum will have heard of *Rocket*, although no doubt some will labour under the misapprehension it was built entirely by George Stephenson, as his son Robert undertook more than his fair share in its production as we shall see. What still never fails to surprise railway enthusiasts is the mistaken belief of many that it was the world's first steam locomotive.

That honour goes to Cornish mining engineer Richard Trevithick, who built a number of steam-powered locomotives firstly for road and then rail, when he found that they were far too heavy for the poor quality muddy potholed roads of the day.

Trevithick successfully demonstrated a steam locomotive in public for the first time on the Penydarren Tramroad near

Towering presence: this statue of George Stephenson watches over all in the National Railway Museum's Great Hall.

Merthyr Tydfil in 1804, but while it clearly impressed the onlookers, it did not immediately spark off a transport technology revolution. Neither did his *Catch-me-who-can* locomotive, which hauled passengers in a carriage around a train set-like circular demonstration track near the site of the present-day Euston Station in 1808.

Indeed, there were plenty of admirers, but for him commercially no takers, and a disillusioned Trevithick moved on to other fields. He died penniless in 1834, ironically the same year at the first steam line in his native Cornwall, the Bodmin & Wadebridge Railway, was opened.

Others, however, had been noting Trevithick's work from afar, even if they had not bought any of his locomotives. In that first decade of steam, the horse was

George Stephenson's first steam locomotive, Blücher.

factories to the nearest canal or harbour relied on equine traction.

However, the Napoleonic Wars generated a massive military demand for horses and their feed, and the resulting shortages back in Britain pushed the price of both up. Hard-pressed colliery owners in the north of England who relied on horses to haul their wagons subsequently took a second glance at Trevithick's ideas, and came to the conclusion that far from being a novelty, a steam locomotive could be made to pay its way commercially.

still the predominant form of general land transport, and the multitude of early railways or tramways laid to link mines and

In 2010 Royal Mail issued a series of stamps marking the 180th anniversary of the opening of the Liverpool & Manchester Railway.

In 1758, the Middleton Railway in Leeds became the first in Britain to be authorised by an Act of Parliament, and as a heritage line it is still very much with us today. In 1812 it became the first commercial railway to successfully use steam locomotives.

Colliery manager John Blenkinsop commissioned engineer Matthew Murray of Fenton, Murray and Wood, in nearby Holbeck, to design a locomotive.

It was based on *Catch-me-who-can*, but used Blenkinsop's innovative rack-and pinion track system, which had a third and toothed rail alongside the usual two to give the locomotive extra adhesion. The engine, named *Salamanca*, improved on Trevithick's design by being the first to use two cylinders. These drove the pinions through cranks at right angles, so that the locomotive would start wherever it came to rest.

The success of *Salamanca* led to other engineers in the north experimenting with their own steam locomotive designs.

George Stephenson was born in Street House in the Northumberland village of Wylam, 9 miles west of Newcastle-upon-Tyne, on 9 June 1781. The infant George, whose family

George Stephenson's boyhood home at Wylam today.

occupied just one of the four rooms in the house, grew up with railways from the outset, for outside the property ran a waggonway linking Wylam Colliery to the River Tyne. It was at Wylam Colliery that *Puffing Billy* ran.

Built in 1813-1814 by engineer William Hedley, engine-wright Jonathan Forster and blacksmith Timothy Hackworth for colliery owner Christopher Blackett, it was the first commercial adhesion steam locomotive, that is, one which ran on two rails and did not require the extra grip provided by Blenkinsop's rack-and-pinion system. *Puffing Billy*, the world's oldest surviving steam locomotive, hauled trains of chaldron wagons containing coal from the colliery to the docks at Lemington-on-Tyne. It was the huge success of *Puffing Billy* that created a demand for more locomotives for the waggonways of the north east, which became known to historians as the 'cradle of the railways'. The name of the engine also entered the English language in phrases like 'puffing like Billy-o'.

Yet the steam locomotive was still seen very much as a machine capable of hauling freight over short local lines, and nobody talked about a national network of railways linking villages, towns and cities.

George was the second child of Robert and Mabel Stephenson, who were both illiterate. Robert was the poorly-paid fireman for the Wylam Colliery pumping engine, and there was no money to pay for sending their children to school.

Accordingly, when he was 17, George became an engineman at Water Row Pit, Newburn, but lamented his lack of education and so paid to learn reading, writing and arithmetic at night school.

He started work at Black Callerton Colliery in 1801 as a 'brakesman', controlling the pit winding gear. The following year, he married Frances (Fanny) Henderson, nine years his senior, and moved to Willington Quay, east of Newcastle, where he took charge of a local colliery's coal-loading apparatus.

The couple lived in one room of a cottage, and George supplemented his income by making shoes and mending clocks. However, he was rapidly developing a passion not only for mechanics but the new steam technology.

On 16 October 1803 their son Robert was born, and the year afterwards they moved to West Moor near Killingworth, George taking a new job as a brakesman at Killingworth Colliery.

Frances gave birth to a daughter, who died after a few weeks, and herself died of tuberculosis in 1806. Left as the sole provider, George sought work in Scotland, leaving Robert with a local woman while he did a job in Montrose. He returned after only a few months, possibly because his father

Dial cottage, George Stephenson's cottage at West Moor.

had been blinded in a mining accident. George moved back into his West Moor cottage and his unmarried sister Eleanor came to look after Robert.

George's big break came in 1811 when the pumping engine at High Pit, Killingworth began failing and he offered to fix it. He was widely praised for his efforts in doing so and they earned him promotion to the position enginewright for all the neighbouring collieries at Killingworth, responsible for maintaining and repairing all of the colliery engines.

His much higher wage allowed him to send Robert to a two-room primary school run by Mr and Mrs Rutter in nearby Longbenton until he was 11.

George Stephenson produced his first railway locomotive in 1814, with the help of Killingworth Colliery manager Nicholas Wood, in the colliery workshop behind his home, Dial Cottage, in Lime Road. He is said to have built a total of 16 while at Killingworth.

A travelling engine designed for hauling coal on the Killingworth waggonway, it was named *Blücher* after the Prussian general Gebhard Leberecht von Blücher. It could haul 30 tons of coal up a hill at 4 miles an hour and was the world's first successful flanged-wheel adhesion steam locomotive that included cylinder rods connected directly to the wheels.

His engines included a six-wheeler built for the Kilmarnock & Troon Railway in 1817 which, however, was quickly withdrawn because it damaged the cast-iron rails on which it ran — a common problem with early steam engines since the time of Trevithick. A locomotive built for Scott's Pit railroad at Llansamlet near Swansea in 1819 also caused damage to the track and had to be taken out of service.

The track problem presented a challenge to George. Steam engines could not run on the traditional wooden rails of horse tramways, and cast iron rails were too brittle.

Joining forces with Tyneside chemist and industrialist William Losh, the pair produced improved cast-iron rails that did not break as easily as existing rails.

George's success in locomotive engineering gave him the ability to enrol Robert in a private educational establishment, Dr Bruce's Academy in Percy Street, Newcastle, where, despite his humble background, he studied alongside the children of well-off families. He failed to impress fellow pupils at the academy, but nonetheless became a reading member of the nearby Literary and Philosophical Society while he was there.

Afterwards, Robert was apprenticed to Nicholas Wood and later attended the University of Edinburgh where he met budding engineer George Parker Bidder.

As a diversion from transport technology, in 1818 George Stephenson looked at ways of preventing the gas explosions caused in mines by naked flames, and came up with a safety that would burn without causing an explosion. A month before scientist Sir Humphry Davy announced he had solved the same problem, with his safety lamp that was to become standard equipment in mines around the world, George demonstrated his own lamp to two witnesses inside Killingworth Colliery. The two inventions differed in that Stephenson's lamp was housed in a glass cylinder while Davy's lamp was surrounded by a gauze screen.

Davy won a prize of £2,000 for his invention, while George, who had developed his lamp with the aid of Wood, was accused of stealing his idea! A committee of inquiry found in George's favour after he proved he had been working independently of Davy and gave him £1,000, but Davy's supporters refused to accept that an uneducated mining engineer could come up with the same solution as an eminent scientist.

Despite their misgivings, a House of Commons committee ruled that George had an equal claim to the invention the safety lamp. Davy died still believing that George had stolen his idea, while George distrusted London scientific experts for the rest of his life. The net result was that George's lamp was used exclusively in the north east, but Davy's lamp was adopted everywhere else.

A story runs that local miners began calling their Stephenson lamps Geordies, deriving from a diminutive form of George, and the use of the name widened to being used for that of the colliers too. Eventually it expanded to the point that any Tyneside native or supporter of Newcastle United FC could be called a Geordie. An alternative explanation is that the nickname dates from the Jacobite Rebellion of 1745, when Newcastle folk were regarded by the Scots as staunch supporters of King George II and the Hanoverian kings, as opposed to rural Northumbrians, who supported the Jacobites.

Davy may have conquered the world outside the north east with his safety lamp, but it was George Stephenson who from inside that region would soon embark on a course that would open up the five continents to the steam railway concept and in doing so reshape the globe forever.

The next pivotal moment came in 1819 when the Hetton Coal Company took on George to build what became known as the Hetton Railway, which ran from Hetton Colliery at Hetton-le-Hole in the Durham coalfield northwards to the coal staithes at Sunderland.

Building of the 8-mile line began in March 1821. The most formidable obstacle facing George was the 636ft high Warden Law, while at Sunderland there were steep cliffs impeding the way to the river. Stephenson's plan for the line included two locomotive-worked sections, two rope inclines worked by stationary engines and five gravity-worked inclines.

It was the first all-new railway to be built by George, but far more importantly, the first in the world to be purpose-designed for use by steam traction.

The line's first five locomotives were built by George between 1820-22, all 0-4-0s with chain-coupled wheels. Four of them had names: *Hetton, Dart, Tallyho* and *Star*. The engine built in 1822 ran in service until around 1913, was last steamed in the 1920s and now known as the 'Hetton locomotive', is displayed in Locomotion: the National Railway Museum at Shildon.

It was by no means all plain sailing. In 1823, a report

stated that on the final part of the northern locomotive-hauled section, a steam engine hauling 16 wagons could manage just 3 miles an hour. When Elemore Colliery was opened in February 1827 and more capacity was needed, a somewhat retrograde step in the story of locomotive development saw the engines replaced with rope haulage. However, the speed increased to 10mph.

George's Hetton Railway was rebuilt on a several occasions before Lord Joicey, the most powerful coal magnate in Durham, bought Hetton Colliery in 1911. The Hetton Railway then became part of his Lambton Railway, another private line, and the combined system became known as the Lambton, Hetton & Joicey Railway.

The piecemeal closure of the Hetton Railway began with its line to North Moor on 9 September 1959, and ended the final section closing on 30 June 1972. The track had all been lifted by March 1973, but the railway had earned its immortal place in history.

Having considerably increased his wealth, George remarried on 29 March 1820, to Betty Hindmarsh, at Newburn, but the couple had no further children.

A month after the building of the Hetton Railway had begun, George the rising star of steam technology had earned himself promotion … to the position as engineer of the new Stockton & Darlington Railway, a line that he had, together with his son Robert, then 18, surveyed the year before.

The Stockton & Darlington was not the first public railway in Britain — that was the Llanelli & Mynydd Mawr Railway in Carmarthenshire, which began running trains in 1803 before the Surrey Iron Railroad, which is often claimed to be the first because it was incorporated a few months earlier. However, the Stockton & Darlington was the world's first public steam-powered railway.

Proposals to link the South West Durham coalfield to the navigable River Tees received serious consideration in 1767, but the scheme ultimately failed to take off.

Left: In 1822, George Stephenson and Nicholas Wood built this 0-4-0 for Hetton Colliery in County Durham. It is now displayed in the Locomotion museum at Shildon.

In 1810, the Recorder of Stockton, Leonard Raisbeck, again suggested building a canal, or maybe a railway, from Stockton through Darlington to the coalfield.

A subsequent proposal was made in 1816 for a canal from Stockton to Darlington and a railway from Darlington to the coalfield near West Auckland was mooted, and civic leaders in Stockton backed it once the plans were unveiled two years later. However, in August 1818 Darlington and Yarm businessmen along with Raisbeck drew up an alternative scheme based solely on a railway. The idea gathered momentum, and by mid-December, the canal scheme was abandoned by the Stockton contingent and an enabling Bill was presented to Parliament.

The Stockton & Darlington Railway Bill was rejected by a

Right: On display inside Newcastle's Stephenson Railway Museum is the Killingworth Billy, built in 1826 to pull coal trains to the staithes on the River Tyne. It was a development of George Stephenson's earlier 'Killingworth Travelling Engine' and last ran under its own power in 1881 to mark the centenary of his birth.

majority of 13 at its first reading in 1819 after the local landed gentry loudly protested. A compromise was eventually reached with alternative routes, based around a 26⅞-mile main line from Stockton to Witton Park with branch lines to Darlington, Yarm, Coundon and Haggerleases Lane. The revised Bill was passed in the House of Lords on 17 April 1821 and received the Royal Assent two days later.

Unlike the private railways that Stephenson had worked on, the Stockton & Darlington was devised as a public railway, just like a road, which anyone could use, provided they paid tolls for the conveyance of freight.

Quaker Edward Pease, a leading wool merchant, was one of its leading proponents. It was he who in 1821 brought in George Stephenson to resurvey the route originally drawn up by Welsh engineer George Overton in 1818.

After his formal appointment as engineer on 22 January 1822, Stephenson convinced Pease that steam haulage was the way ahead.

The new railway was inaugurated at St John's Well, Stockton, when company chairman Thomas Meynell cut the first sod and laid the first rails 4ft 8in apart.

That measurement itself had resounding consequences for the world's railways.

George Stephenson worked out that measurement from the average gap between the wheels of the horse-drawn wagons of the day, which would be adapted for use on the new railway. It is believed to derive from the historical practice of placing the wheels of horse-drawn vehicles 5ft apart in order to fit a cart horse between the shafts.

Like the Hetton Railway, the Stockton & Darlington used 4ft 8in gauge for the first 15 years, and was then switched to 4ft 8½in, to comply with subsequent railways and ensure interchangeability of rolling stock. It was 4ft 8½in gauge that subsequently became the norm for Britain's rapidly-growing railway network, although it took until 1892 to completely oust Isambard Kingdom Brunel's one-time rival 7ft 0¼in broad gauge. The gauge was adopted across the globe and became known as 'standard gauge': 60 per cent of the world's railways use it.

A second Stockton & Darlington Railway Bill was submitted

to Parliament in 1823, requesting deviations from the original line and for an additional branch line from Hill House to Croft Bridge, and permission for the conveyance of passengers by steam power. It received the Royal Assent on 23 May.

One of the key features of the railway was the Gaunless Bridge, designed by George and built in 1823 in wrought and cast iron by John and Isaac Burrell of Newcastle.

A manufacturer was needed to build locomotives for the railway, so Pease and George Stephenson jointly established a company in Newcastle for this purpose. It was established as Robert Stephenson and Company, with Robert and as the managing director and Michael Longridge, owner of Bedlington Ironworks, as the fourth partner. One of the works' managers was James Kennedy, who later became, like both Stephensons, president of the Institute of Mechanical Engineers.

George was always very close to his son, who was only 20 years his junior. However, Robert was to miss the opening of the Stockton & Darlington, because in 1824 he went to South America for three years, to work as an engineer in the Colombian gold mines.

Meanwhile, the works in Forth Street completed the first locomotive for the railway in September 1825. At first named *Active*, it was soon renamed *Locomotion No 1* and was followed by *Hope, Diligence* and *Black Diamond*. The firm also agreed to supply two stationary engines, at Etherley and Brusselton.

The track itself used wrought-iron rails produced by John Birkinshaw at Bedlington Ironworks. They had the big advantages over the earlier cast-iron railways devised by George Stephenson and William Losh in that they were far less likely to fracture under the weight of steam locomotives and could be produced in much longer lengths.

Losh was bitterly disappointed because he believed he had an agreement with George Stephenson to use his rails and the pair fell out permanently.

In 1825, Timothy Hackworth was taken on as the railway's the first locomotive superintendent, taking the place of George Stephenson, who was now engaged on the Liverpool & Manchester Railway project and away for much of the time.

On 17 September that year, *Locomotion No 1* was taken

The official opening of the Stockton & Darlington Railway on 27 August 1825.

A contemporary sketch of the Stockton & Darlington Railway in 1825.

from Newcastle on a horse-drawn waggon and positioned on the track at Aycliffe Lane, later Heighington Station.

Once positioned on the track, its fire was lit by the sun through Darlington resident Robert Metcalfe's magnifying glass. He always carried it with him and had it handy when George Stephenson needed a lighted lantern.

The railway company's official carriage, *Experiment*, arrived from Newcastle on 26 September 1825 and attached to

Locomotion No 1 at Shildon before several directors, including Pease and George Stephenson, enjoyed a trial run to Darlington.

Early the next day, 12 waggons filled with coal were taken to the foot of the Etherley incline, where they were drawn up and lowered down to St Helen's level crossing. After a waggon loaded with flour was added to the train, it was hauled by horse traction across the Gaunless Bridge to the foot of the Brusselton incline, where some passengers, mainly labourers who had built the railway, boarded. To the delight of a large crowd, the waggons were hauled up by the Brusselton engine and lowered down to Shildon Lane End where *Locomotion No 1* simmered in steam.

The Stockton & Darlington Railway's first locomotive was Locomotion No 1, built in George and Robert Stephenson's works under Timothy Hackworth, and now displayed inside Head of Steam – Darlington Railway Museum.

From this point, *Locomotion No 1* hauled 21 waggons fitted with seats along with *Experiment*, as a procession led by a man on horseback bearing a flag. The history-making train arrived Darlington inside two hours having recorded an average speed of 8mph.

There, more waggons including two carrying the Yarm Brass Band were added to the train. A total of 31 vehicles and 550 passengers were then conveyed to Stockton to a civic reception six hours later. It was the first time that passengers had been officially carried on a public steam railway.

However, the Stockton & Darlington was not the world's first railway to offer timetabled steam-hauled passenger trains, for in its first few years, these services were still horse drawn, still a cheaper alternative to steam, and run by private operators. The Canterbury & Whitstable Railway, which opened on 3 May 1830, and largely comprised cable-hauled inclines, operated steam-hauled passenger services from the outset. Its first locomotive, *Invicta*, named after the motto on the Flag of Kent, was the 20th locomotive built by Robert Stephenson & Company. It was withdrawn as early as 1839 and is

Beamish Museum in County Durham produced a working replica of Locomotion No 1 in 1975.

Invicta, *the locomotive built by Robert Stephenson &
Company immediately after Rocket, and now in the
Canterbury Museum.*

considered to be the world's first steam locomotive to be
officially preserved, and is currently on display in Canterbury
Museum. A new museum at Whitstable to house *Invicta* and a
stationary winding engine built at Robert Stephenson's works
has been planned.

After several years the economic potential for carrying
passengers became clear and the Stockton & Darlington
introduced its own steam passenger services in 1833.

Hackworth went on to establish a locomotive works at
Shildon, and became a key player in the development of the
steam locomotive.

Meanwhile, the boiler of *Locomotion No 1* exploded in
1828, killing its driver. The engine was rebuilt at overhaul at
the Shildon works, and remained in service until 1841, when
it was bought by Joseph Pease and partners for use as a
pumping engine. It is now displayed in Head of Steam –
Darlington Railway Museum alongside a later Stockton &
Darlington locomotive, Derwent.

The Stockton & Darlington built a larger locomotive works
at Shildon in 1833. The railway was eventually taken over by

St John's Well, No 48 Bridge Road, Stockton, was the original eastern passenger terminus of the Stockton & Darlington Railway and is said to be the world's first ticket office.

Right: An original Stockton & Darlington Railway coach preserved at Beamish Museum. Note the similarity of its design to that of a stagecoach of the day.

Lengths of original Stockton & Darlington Railway track in the Head of Steam Museum.

a bigger company, the North Eastern Railway, in 1863, but not until it had expanded throughout west Durham and Teesside by a series of new lines, amalgamations and takeovers, eventually running to Penrith on the far side of the Pennines via the legendary route over Stainmore Summit. A branch opened in 1830 led to the development of a new town, Middlesbrough, which mushroomed as a major industrial centre. A further extension, through a separate company promoted by the railway, took the line to Saltburn, which another associated company developed as a seaside resort.

Robert Stephenson in his younger days.

A far bigger 'first' was George Stephenson's next major project.

The Liverpool & Manchester Railway was the world's first inter-city passenger railway. It was designed to facilitate the cheap and efficient transport of raw materials and finished goods between Liverpool docks and east Lancashire.

One principal trade target was the huge quantities of raw materials for textiles imported through Liverpool for the mills near the Pennines where water and then steam power enabled the production of the finished cloth. There was general unhappiness at the excessive profits made by the existing means of water transport, the Mersey and Irwell Navigation and the Bridgewater Canal, and the fact that they were said to be stifling the growth of Manchester and other towns.

Both cities wanted to be linked by a railway, but as was the case with so many early schemes, landowners in the middle objected. The main promoters were John Kennedy, owner of the biggest spinning mill in Manchester, and Liverpool corn merchant Joseph Sandars. Bending their ear was William James, a largely-overlooked figure who some historians claim was the true father of the railways, not George Stephenson.

James, a land surveyor who had earned a fortune through property speculation, was a proponent of a national network of railways, taking the steam locomotive concept he had witnessed in the north east several stages further.

The Liverpool & Manchester Railway Company was founded on 24 May 1823 by Henry Booth, who became its secretary and treasurer, along with other merchants from both cities. James made the first survey of the line, but it was held to be defective, and he became bankrupt. In 1824, George Stephenson was appointed engineer in his place, but was taking on too much work, and delegated much of the work to others.

A Bill presented in 1825 to Parliament was thrown out, after George's survey was shown to be inaccurate.

The railway promoters then replaced him with brothers George and John Rennie, the sons of canal engineer John

Railway engineer John Rennie.

Rennie the Elder, as engineers. In turn, they chose ex-army engineer Charles Blacker Vignoles as their surveyor.

The railway promoters then made peace with major opponents including the canal lobby which included G. H. Bradshaw, one of the trustees of the Marquess of Stafford's Worsley estate, which included the Bridgewater Canal. They also drew on the support of Liverpool MP William Huskisson, president of the Board of Trade and treasurer of the Royal Navy. Soon, opposition to the railway was converted into financial support!

A second Bill was passed by Parliament, received the Royal Assent in 1826, and involved a different and more difficult 35-mile route. The biggest obstacle was the crossing of Chat Moss, a peat bog that comprised a third of the Salford area.

The Mersey and Irwell Navigation withdrew its opposition to the railway crossing the river at the last moment, after

An 1831 Thomas Bury print depicting the excavation of Olive Mount Cuitting on the Liverpool & Manchester Railway. More than 480,000 cubic yards of sandstone rock had to be removed to make the 2-mile long cutting. The rock was used to build the Roby embankment and Sankey Viaduct.

reaching an agreement for its carts to have access to the bridge. As a result, the Manchester terminus was pencilled in for a site at Liverpool Road in the heart of Castlefield.

The railway company then failed to agree to the high terms being demanded by the Rennie brothers, and so George Stephenson was reappointed as engineer with his young assistant Joseph Locke, who at first worked alongside Vignoles. However, a clash of personalities with George Stephenson led to Vignoles resigning leaving Locke in sole charge.

The line began with the 2,250-yard Edge Hill or Wapping Tunnel which ran from the south end of Liverpool Docks to Edge Hill. It was the world's first tunnel to be bored under a city.

After this came a 2-mile cutting up to 70ft-deep hacked by hand through rock at Olive Mount, and the nine-arch Sankey Brook Viaduct, each arch having a 50ft span. The most famous feat of all, however, was the 43.4-mile crossing of Chat Moss.

George Stephenson wanted to drain the bog, but came to the conclusion it was impossible. Instead, an ingenious method of 'floating' the railway across the bog was used.

George Stephenson's Sankey Viaduct, which took the world's first inter-city steam railway over the Sankey Canal, the first canal of the Industrial Revolution.

A large number of wooden and heather hurdles were sunk into the bog and covered with earth and stones to give a solid foundation. The solution was so effective that the line over the bog carries today's far heavier trains without difficulty, although you can feel the ground move as one passes.

One of the shafts of Liverpool's Edge Hill or Wapping Tunnel.

Locke, who had responsibility for the western half of the line, was believed to have come up with the solution to the bog problem, although George Stephenson usually gets the credit for it.

Altogether, the railway had 64 bridges and viaducts. All of them were traditionally built from brick or masonry, apart from the Water Street Bridge at the Manchester terminus. Here, a cast-iron beam girder bridge designed by William Fairbairn and Eaton Hodgkinson, and cast locally at their factory in Ancoats was used to save headway in the street below the line. This bridge set a precedent for similar bridges to be used all over the national rail network that was to follow in the decades ahead.

At Rainhill, a skew bridge, the first bridge in the world to cross any railway at an angle, was erected. A listed structure, it is still in use at Rainhill Station and carries traffic on the A57 Warrington Road.

The gauge for the double-track railway was George Stephenson's 4ft 8½in, half an inch wider than his original Stockton & Darlington gauge.

While the line was under construction, the company directors could not reach a decision as to the best method of traction. Should stationary engines hauling the trains along by cables be used instead of steam locomotives?

It was a quarter of a century since Trevithick had given his first public demonstration of one, but locomotives relying on adhesion had not until this point proved entirely reliable. Indeed, there had been failures on the Stockton & Darlington, and part of the Hetton Railway had been converted to cable haulage.

Also, the railway company had tried to play down the mention of locomotives during the enabling Bill's passage through Parliament, because of public fears that they would either explode or suffocate everyone with poisonous fumes.

Robert Stephenson, who was now back in Britain running his Newcastle works, and Locke remained convinced that locomotives were the way forward, (the breakdown of a stationary engine on a cable-hauled system would paralyse the whole line) and in March 1829 presented a report arguing their case to the directors — who then decided to hold an open

The Rainhill Trials of 1829 were 'restaged' at the Llangollen Railway in 2002 for the BBC TV programme Timewatch – Rocket and its Rivals, using modern-day replicas. The winner of both the original and the 'replay' was Rocket: the replica of which is seen next to that of Novelty.

trial to find the best locomotive. This was the Rainhill Trials of 1829, a seminal point in the history of world railway evolution.

A £500 prize was offered to the winner of the trials, and three key figures from the early railway age were chosen as judges: the aforementioned Killingworth Colliery manager and locomotive designer Nicholas Wood, Stourbridge locomotive engineer John Urpeth Rastrick and Manchester cotton spinner and railway supporter John Kennedy.

The locomotives were to be subjected to a series of tests, including ten trips equal to a total of 35 miles, with 30 of them performed at full speed, with an average of at least 10mph – two miles faster than the Stockton & Darlington at that time.

Ten locomotives were entered, but when the contest began on 6 October, only five took part.

The first to drop out was Thomas Shaw Brandreth's *Cycloped*, which used a horse walking on a drive belt to power it. It came to grief when the horse burst through the floor of the engine following an accident, and may be considered equine traction's 'last stand' as far as railways are concerned (although horses were still used for shunting at Newmarket until 1967).

The next to fail was *Perseverance*, built by Timothy Burstall, which was withdrawn after failing to reach the necessary 10mph. Nevertheless, it was given a £25 consolation prize.

Timothy Hackworth's *Sans Pareil*, which had been criticised as being overweight, completed eight round trips before a cylinder cracked and it too was withdrawn. However, it sufficiently impressed to be bought by the railway, which ran it for two years before leasing it to the Bolton and Leigh Railway.

Novelty, built by John Ericsson and John Braithwaite, was markedly faster than the other entrants and won the hearts of the large crowd. It reached a then jaw-dropping 28mph on its debut, but problems with a boiler pipe later damaged it to the extent it too had to be withdrawn. In 1833 *Novelty* was rebuilt by Robert Daglish and supplied to the St Helens & Runcorn Gap Railway.

The only locomotive to finish the competition was the Stephensons' *Rocket*.

Vintage models of Rainhills Trials competitors
Rocket, Novelty *and* Sans Pareil *at the National Railway Museum in York.*

An 0-2-2, with a pair of driving wheels and a pair of trailing wheels, it was built by Robert Stephenson and Company especially for the trials.

Its global importance is that it brought together several advances in locomotive technology to produce the most advanced engine of its day, and formed the template for most steam locomotives since. The textbook steam engine design is often referred to as the Stephensonian locomotive.

Its features included a multi-tubular boiler, which made for much more efficient and effective heat transfer between the exhaust gases and the water. Before *Rocket*, locomotive boilers consisted of a single pipe surrounded by water.

The firebox was separate from the boiler and was built to double thickness, being surrounded with water. Copper pipes led the heated water into the boiler, where 25 copper tubes running the full length carried the hot exhaust gases from the firebox. This innovation hugely boosted the amount of steam produced, and accordingly, all future locomotive designs featured increased numbers of boiler tubes. It has been said that Henry Booth, the treasurer of the Liverpool & Manchester Railway, came up with the idea of the multi-tube boiler, based on a design by French engineer Marc Seguin that provided improved heat exchange, and suggested it to Robert Stephenson.

Rocket also had a blastpipe, feeding the exhaust steam from the cylinders into the base of the chimney in order induce a partial vacuum and pull air through the fire. The blastpipe concept, developed by both Sir Goldsworthy Gurney and Hackworth, was unsuccessful on earlier locomotive designs as it tended to rip the top off the fire and throw burning cinders out of the chimney, enormously increasing the fuel consumption. However, it was ideal for *Rocket's* multi-tube boiler.

Rocket's two cylinders were originally set at 35 degrees from the horizontal, with the pistons driving a pair of 4ft 8in diameter wheels. Most previous locomotive designs had the cylinders positioned vertically, which caused an uneven swaying motion as locomotives moved forward. Rocket was later modified so that the cylinders were set horizontally, a feature used on nearly all designs in its wake.

Yet who designed *Rocket* — was it the father or the son?

The National Railway Museum's static replica of Rocket inside the Great Hall.

No engine devised by George Stephenson up to this point had been anything like as advanced as *Rocket*. Indeed, while it was being designed and built in Newcastle, he was overseeing the construction of the Liverpool & Manchester.

While George is popularly credited with producing *Rocket*, it was Robert who was left in charge of its design and construction, although he regularly communicated with his father. Logic dictates it was Robert, therefore, who carried out most of the work.

On 17 June 1829, Robert married Frances Sanderson in London. The couple went to live at 5 Greenfield Place, off Westgate Road in Newcastle.

The grand opening of the Liverpool & Manchester took place on 15 September 1830, and was attended by government and leading industry figures, including the Prime Minister, the Duke of Wellington.

The event began with a parade of eight trains setting out from Liverpool, led by locomotive *Northumbrian* driven by George Stephenson. *Northumbrian* was the last of the Stephensons' Rocket-style 0-2-2s but featured a number of improvements, notably the inclusion of the Stephenson-type firebox incorporated in the boiler, and a smokebox that was the full diameter of the boiler. In this respect, *Northumbrian* may be considered to have had the first true 'locomotive' boiler. It also had plate frames and a proper tender.

The parade included *Phoenix* driven by Robert, *North Star* driven by George's brother Robert Senior and *Rocket* driven by Locke. *Phoenix* and *North Star* had also been supplied by Robert Stephenson & Company to the Rocket design and had larger cylinders.

Both the day and *Rocket's* appearance were marred by tragedy, in the form of the world's first public railway fatality. After the VIP group enjoyed a ride on *Northumbrian*, MP William Huskisson walked over the track from his own carriage to speak to the Duke of Wellington. By-standers shouted warnings that *Rocket*, driven by Locke, was about to pass *Northumbrian* but Huskisson realised the danger too late. Unable to move clear in time, he was knocked down by *Rocket* and one of his legs was badly mangled. His first words, on being lifted off the track, were "I have met my death." which unhappily proved true. A doctor attempted to stem the bleeding and George Stephenson used *Northumbrian* to take him 15 miles in 25 minutes, at 36mph, for further treatment — the world's first ambulance train. However, Huskisson died later that day in Eccles parsonage.

Because of the large crowds that had gathered along the line between Liverpool and Manchester to witness the

Opening day on the Liverpool & Manchester Railway.

The National Railway Museum's working replica of Rocket, built in 1980 by engineer Mike Satow and Locomotive Enterprises in 1979 for the Rainhill 150th anniversary celebrations. In 2009 it was completely rebuilt by Victorian locomotive restoration experts at Bill Parker's Flour Mill Colliery workshops at Bream in the Forest of Dean, and is seen in action with a matching train on the Great Central Railway.

proceedings, it was decided to continue with the procession despite the tragedy.

However, when *Northumbrian* entered Manchester, weavers hurled stones at the carriages, remembering only too well the Duke of Wellington's involvement in the Peterloo Massacre at the city's St Peter's Field on 16 August 1819, when cavalry charged into a crowd of 60,000–80,000 gathered at a meeting to demand the reform of parliamentary representation and 18 people died from sabre cuts and trampling, as well as

The original Rocket *inside the Science Museum.*

A replica Liverpool & Manchester Railway coach in the National Railway Museum.

his strong opposition to the proposed 1832 Reform Act. Nevertheless, the world's first inter-city railway was an overnight success. In 1831 the company carried 445,047 passengers, taking receipts of £155,702 with profits of £71,098. By 1844 receipts had reached £258,892 with profits of £136,688. During this time shareholders were regularly paid out an annual dividend of £10 for every £100 invested.

A nineteenth-century sketch of Rocket.

By now, the rapid evolution of locomotive design and technology meant that *Rocket* was quickly rendered obsolete as train weights increased.

In 1830, Robert Stephenson & Company produced a 2-2-0, *Planet*, which looked remarkably different to *Rocket* and much like the 'modern' steam locomotives that we are familiar with. It was the first locomotive to employ inside cylinders, a steam dome to prevent water reaching the cylinders, and buffers and couplings in a position that established a new standard.

In 1834, *Rocket* was selected for modifications to test a newly-developed rotary steam engine designed by Admiral Thomas Cochrane, the tenth Earl of Dundonald. *Rocket's* cylinders and driving rods were removed and two of the engines installed directly on its driving axle with a feedwater pump in between. However, an operational trial that October proved a disappointment, as the modified locomotive could not pull a train of empty carriages. Lord Dundonald's engines were thus deemed a feeble failure.

Rocket was placed in storage, but in 1836 was sold to the Earl of Carlisle's railway in Cumberland, where it hauled coal trains. In 1838 it was sold to J. Thompson, another mine owner, who ran it until its withdrawal two years later.

In 1851 it was returned to the Newcastle factory in the hope

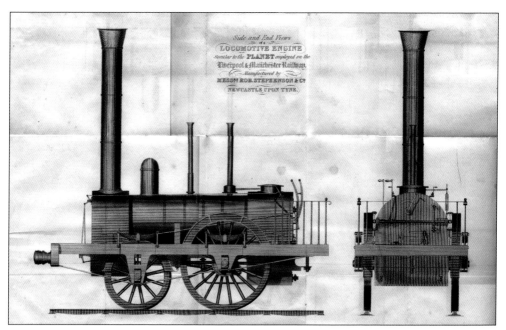

An engraving of Robert Stephenson's Planet *locomotive by William Miller.*

it could be restored for display at the Great Exhibition of 1851 at the Crystal Palace in London, but this never happened. In 1862 *Rocket* was donated to the Patent Office Museum (later the Science Museum) in London by the Thompsons. However, it was hardly recognisable from the locomotive that has won the Rainhill Trials, having undergone several repairs following minor accidents in Liverpool & Manchester service and also many modifications. Science Museum visitors today cannot but fail to notice the great disparity between the copper hulk that remains of *Rocket* and the bright yellow locomotive of paintings, replicas and models.

Around the time that the Liverpool & Manchester was being completed, both Stephensons became involved in the Leicester & Swannington Railway, which received its Royal Assent in 1830 with the first part being opened on 17 July 1832 to carry coal from pits in west Leicestershire to Leicester.

In 1828, Leicester mining engineer William Stenson, who founded Whitwick Colliery, had approached George Stephenson about becoming involved. He not only agreed but helped raise a substantial part of the finance involved through

The Museum of Science & Industry in Manchester has a working replica of Planet, It is seen at Loughborough Station during a gala visit to the Great Central Railway in May 2010.

The Museum of Science & Industry includes the Liverpool & Manchester Railway's Liverpool Road terminus. In February 2010, Prince Charles is seen inspecting the replica of Planet during a visit.

Right: *The replica* Planet *gets up a head of steam on the Great Central Railway.*

his contacts in Liverpool.

Robert Stephenson was appointed engineer. Like many early railways, the Leicester & Swannington was modelled largely on early canals, having flat sections linked by inclined planes, as opposed to locks.

Robert Stephenson & Company built five locomotives for the railway. The opening train was hauled by 0-4-0 *Comet*, and was driven by George Stephenson himself. *Comet's* 13ft high chimney was knocked down by Glenfield Tunnel, due to the track having been packed up too high. It is said that the train stopped so that the passengers could wash themselves in nearby Rothley Brook.

The tunnel was only the second to be built on a passenger railway anywhere in the world, the first being one on the Canterbury & Whitstable Railway which had opened shortly before. Glenfield Tunel was viewed as a marvel by local residents and gates had to be fitted to prevent visits by the curious.

The remainder of the line to Swannington opened in 1833. George Stephenson relocated to Ravenstone near Ashby-de-la-Zouch and with Robert opened a colliery at Snibston in 1833.

Samson, a Robert Stephenson 0-4-2 which arrived in 1833, collided with a horse and cart carrying a load of butter and eggs on its way to Leicester Market. The locomotive's horn had not been loud enough to warn of the impending peril, and so the line's engines were subsequently fitted with the world's first steam whistles.

By 1834, soaring traffic levels needed more powerful locomotives, and so *Atlas*, the first-ever 0-6-0 inside cylinder engine, was built., While inside cylinders were more difficult to build and maintain, locomotives fitted with them were found to be more stable than their outside-cylindered counterparts. The design was so successful that it formed a template for a multitude of freight locomotives over the next century.

The directors of the Leicester & Swannington Railway sold out to the Midland Railway in 1845.

Following the huge success of the Liverpool & Manchester, George Stephenson was besieged with offers of work from other railway promoters.

He worked with Locke on the Grand Junction Railway. Receiving its Royal Assent on 6 May 1833, the 82-mile Grand

Junction opened on 4 July 1837, running from Birmingham through Wolverhampton, Stafford, Crewe, and Warrington and via the existing Warrington & Newton Railway (which had been engineered by Robert Stephenson) to join the Liverpool and Manchester at a triangular junction at Newton Junction. The Grand Junction established its chief engineering works at Crewe, moving there from Edge Hill.

The railway's principal engineering feature was the 20-arch Dutton Viaduct which crossed the River Weaver, and which George Stephenson always claimed to be one of his finest designs, although its construction was supervised by Locke.

On the same day as the Grand Junction received its Royal Assent, so did the London & Birmingham Railway, which had appointed Robert Stephenson as engineer.

It seemed at first as if the father and son would engineer the first railway linking London, Birmingham and Liverpool and Manchester, but it did not turn out as planned for the pair.

The Grand Junction was the first trunk railway to be completed in England, and has also been hailed the world's first long-distance railway with steam traction.

Yet history records that it was not a great personal success for George Stephenson, for his estimates and organising ability paled in comparison with those of Locke. George quit after the board of directors became dissatisfied with him, and a rift between him and Locke was never healed.

Left: A restored porcelain statuette of Robert Stephenson dating from 1859 now displayed inside the National Railway Museum at York.

The London & Birmingham Railway's Camden Town locomotive works and the twin 133ft high chimneys of Robert Stephenson's underground stationary engine winding house.

George Stephenson also worked on railway magnate George Hudson's York & North Midland route from Normanton to York, the Birmingham & Derby, the Manchester & Leeds, and the Sheffield & Rotherham railways.

Many of the pioneering American railroad builders came to Britain for advice from George Stephenson, and several of the first locomotives to run regularly in the USA were bought from Robert Stephenson & Company. The first, an 0-4-0 named *America*, was ordered by the Delaware & Hudson Railroad, and it was followed by an 0-6-0 named *Whistler* and supplied to the Boston & Providence Railroad in 1833. Later renamed *Massachusetts*, it was lost in a bog in Mansfield, Massachusetts.

Another railway he engineered, but without steam locomotives, was the horse-worked Whitby & Pickering Railway. Following the success of the Stockton & Darlington Railway, Whitby traders looked at the possibility of having a line serving their port, and in 1832, George was asked to draw up a plan. The Whitby & Pickering Railway Bill received Royal Assent from William IV on 6 May 1833.

*The Avon Viaduct on the
London & Birmingham Railway.*

George engineered a 1,500-yard-long rope-worked incline at an average gradient of 1-in-15 to take the line up from the valley of the Murk Esk at Beckhole to the high moors at Goathland. He also crossed Fen Bog, near the summit of the line, using the same techniques he employed at Chat Moss.

The line was absorbed into the York & North Midland Railway in 1845 and rebuilt as a double track steam-worked railway. It was extended to meet the new owner's York to Scarborough line at Rillington Junction.

The line from Rillington Junction to Whitby was closed under the Beeching Axe, but the section north of Pickering has been revived by enthusiasts. The North Yorkshire Moors Railway, as it is now known, runs regular services over the Network Rail section of the Esk Valley line into Whitby, and helped somewhat by the publicity it received through its appearances on the TV 1960s' police drama series *Heartbeat*, is today Britain's most popular heritage railway, carrying more than 330,000 passengers in 2010.

George Stephenson began focusing on his mining and quarrying interests in Derbyshire, after his tunnelling work for the North Midland Railway in the 1830s revealed new coal seams.

He chose Crich Cliff Quarry near Matlock to supply limestone for his iron-smelting businesses. The stone was transported via a mineral railway to kilns at Ambergate alongside the 72-mile North Midland Railway that he had engineered from Derby to Rotherham and Leeds.

George Stephenson decided to build this short mineral railway not to his 4ft 8½in standard gauge, but to metre gauge. While narrow gauge offers the advantage of being able to cross more circuitous and hilly terrain, nobody knows exactly why he chose metre gauge. One story is that he employed a team of

The original route of George Stephenson's 1835 Whitby & Pickering Railway at Moorgates.

An 1836 painting of a Whitby & Pickering Railway horse-drawn service passing Tunnel Inn.

Dutch engineers to build the line, and after he merely told them to use narrow gauge, they selected a metre, the standard measurement on the continent, on the assumption that it was as good as any other. It was the first metre gauge railway in the world.

Metre gauge never caught on big time in Britain, and there is no evidence to suggest that George Stephenson thought it might: the best-known lines that used it were to be found in the Northamptonshire ironstone quarries. However, metre gauge became widely used throughout the rest of the world.

In several African, American and Asian countries it is still the predominant gauge. On the

A section of track has been laid on the Leicester & Swannington Railway near Coalville as a memorial to Stephenson's line.

This stationary steam winding engine, built by Robert Stephenson in 1833, served the Leicester & Swannington Railway, hauling wagons up the 1-in-17 Swannington incline. It remained in use until 1947 and is now in the National Railway Museum.

continent, it was used for local railways in France, Germany, and Belgium, but after most of these closed in the mid-twentieth century, only Switzerland and northern Spain still have sizeable metre gauge networks in regular use, although many European urban tram systems run on metre gauge tracks.

While building the North Midland Railway, he took a liking to Chesterfield, and leased Tapton House. The late eighteenth-century property had been constructed by the Wilkinson family, bankers who also helped finance the building of the Chesterfield Canal.

By the time he was appointed as the first president of the Institution of Mechanical Engineers on its formation in 1847, George Stephenson had become semi retired. On 11 January 1848, at St John's church in Shrewsbury, George married for the third time, to farmer's daughter Ellen Gregory, who had been his housekeeper.

Six months after the wedding, George contracted pleurisy and died aged 67 on 12 August 1848 at Tapton House.

He was buried alongside his second wife at Holy Trinity church in Newbold Road, Chesterfield, where he had been a regular worshipper. The grave is marked only by a rough slab of Derbyshire stone flooring on which the legend 'G. S. 1848' has been carved.

A bronze statue of George Stephenson was unveiled at Chesterfield Station on 28 October 2005. His portrait also appeared on Bank of England £5 notes between 1990 and 2003.

The quarry served by his metre gauge railway is now home to Crich Tramway Village, home of the National Tramway Museum, where a vast collection of street trams can be seen in service on tracks laid through a series of cameo street scenes.

Robert Stephenson continued the family tradition of shaping the world of railways.

For the London & Birmingham Railway, which had been first proposed by John Rennie in 1823, he selected a route through Coventry, to avoid possible flooding from the River Thames at Oxford. Much of the finance came from Lancashire, where rich mill owners were eager to find a wider market for their cotton products.

Construction began in November 1833 with the first part of the line, between Euston and Boxmoor (Hemel Hempstead) opening on 20 July 1837. Stephenson oversaw the construction of the tunnel beneath Primrose Hill, which needed excavation by shafts.

In 1834, Robert Stephenson offered George Parker Bidder, his old friend from Edinburgh, a position on the railway. Two years later, Bidder began helping George Stephenson in schemes for railways between London and Brighton and between Manchester and Rugby via the Potteries. Bidder went

A stone workshop built for George Stephenson's metre gauge mineral railway at Crich, now part of Crich Tramway Village.

on to become a renowned railway engineer in his own right, while helping Robert on other schemes.

Delays caused by building Kilsby Tunnel in Northamptonshire meant that the London & Birmingham Railway could not open in time for Queen Victoria's coronation on 28 June 1838. The railway, the first main line to enter London, was formally opened throughout on 17 September 1838.

Because the locomotives provided for the line by the firm of Bury proved inadequate to tackle the Camden Bank incline from Euston to Camden Town, stationary winding engines in an engine house built by Robert Stephenson hauled the trains up by rope from October 1837 until 1844. Trains were drawn up by an endless rope that ran around a 20ft driving wheel. The rope was 3,744 yards long, seven inches in circumference and weighed 12 tons.

Robert Stephenson.

The railway established its own locomotive workshops at the halfway point of Wolverton in 1838.

In 1846, the London & Birmingham amalgamated with the Grand Junction and the Manchester & Birmingham to form the London & North Western Railway.

The grandiose Curzon Street terminus in Birmingham closed to passenger traffic in 1854 although the original building survives, but Euston Station was demolished in 1962 to make way for a modern replacement.

As with his father, Robert's fame and fortune spread far and wide, and he was offered jobs overseas. After his success in overseeing the building of the Leopolda Railway in Tuscany in 1838, Russian princes Anatolio Demidoff and Giuseppe Poniatowski asked him to construct a railway to Forlì, passing through the Muraglione Pass. This line was never built, but paved the way for the Faentina Railway which was constructed four decades later.

He advised French engineer Paulin Talabot on the building of the Chemins de fer du Gard from Beaucaire to Alès during 1837-1840, and provided expertise during the construction of the Spanish railway from the Bay of Biscay to Madrid. In 1846, Robert and Talabot also studied the feasibility of building a Suez canal. Between 1851-53, he oversaw the construction of the Alexandria to Cairo railway, which was extended to Suez in 1858. Robert was also summoned in 1850 by the Swiss Federal Council to advise on the development of the Swiss railway system.

With the success of the Stephenson railways, the Newcastle locomotive works expanded and continued to prosper.

However, Robert Stephenson was still prepared to use non-locomotive technology for new railway schemes. Appointed as engineer to the London & Blackwall Railway, he was compelled not only to follow the route surveyed by John Rennie because it had been rubber stamped by Parliament in 1836, but also use the obscure track gauge of 5ft 0¼in. He drew on

The London & Birmingham Railway's original Curzon Street terminus.

A sketch of Curzon Street Station in 1838.

his experience with Camden Bank and decided to use cable rather than locomotive haulage and stationary steam engines. The line opened on 6 July 1840, and the line was converted to steam locomotive operation and standard gauge eight years later.

At his Newcastle works, the Stephenson valve gear or Stephenson link or shifting link, a simple design of valve gear that became widely used throughout the world for all kinds of steam engine, was invented, but although it was named after Robert, it was devised in 1842 by two of his workers, draughtsman William Howe and pattern-maker William Williams.

Also, the company tackled problems with the fireboxes and chimneys caused by the increased distance travelled by many trains. With the aid of the North Midland Railway's Derby works, Robert measured the temperature of the exhaust gases, and decided to lengthen the boilers on future engines.

The first 'long-boiler' engines were 2-2-2 types, but in 1844, Robert moved the trailing wheel to the front in 4-2-0 formation, so that the cylinders could be mounted between the supporting wheels. In 1846 he added a pair of trailing wheels, creating the first locomotives with eight wheels.

The company also built several 4-2-0s for the South Eastern Railway and the London, Chatham & Dover Railway.

Robert also followed in his father's footsteps in the field of bridge construction. For the York, Newcastle & Berwick Railway, he designed the High Level Bridge, at Newcastle as a two-deck bridge supported on tall stone columns, with rail traffic carried on the upper deck and road traffic on the lower deck.

He also designed the 28-arch Royal Border Bridge over the River Tweed for the York, Newcastle & Berwick. When Victoria opened it in 1850, passengers could travel from London to Edinburgh by the same railway line for the first time.

That year, Robert and Scottish civil engineer, structural engineer and shipbuilder William Fairbairn completed the Britannia Bridge across the Menai Strait, linking Anglesey to the mainland. Its innovative design featuring wrought-iron box-section tubes to carry railway tracks inside them.

The tubular design using wrought-iron to provide the ultimate in strength and flexibility was first used with

High Level Bridge in Newcastle-upon-Tyne.

resounding effect on the Conwy railway bridge between Llandudno Junction and Conwy two years earlier.

Despite its comparatively high expense, Robert adapted this design for other bridges, the 6,588ft Victoria Bridge over the St Lawrence River at Montreal in Canada, and two in Egypt.

His other successful bridges include a joint road and rail bridge in 1850 over the River Nene, at Sutton Bridge in Lincolnshire, which carried the Midland & Great Northern Joint Railway main line until the system's closure in 1959, and now is part of the A17 between Sleaford and King's Lynn, and the Ulverston & Lancaster Railway's Arnside Viaduct across the River Kent in Cumbria.

However, one spectacular failure was the Dee Bridge near Chester, which collapsed on 24 May 1847 as a local train from Ruabon ran over it and fell through, leaving three passengers, the train guard, and the fireman, dead.

Robert designed it using cast-iron girders, each of which was made of three very large castings dovetailed together. Each girder was strengthened by wrought-iron bars.

The bridge was completed in September 1846, and opened

Border Bridge which takes today's East Coast Main Line across the River Tweed.

for local traffic after approval by the first Railway Inspector, General Charles Pasley.

Robert was accused of negligence at a local inquest, because cast iron was known to be brittle in tension or bending.

The investigation into the disaster was one of the first major inquiries conducted by the newly-formed Railway Inspectorate. A report submitted by lead investigator Captain John Lintorn

The tubular rail bridge at Conwy.

John Lucas' painting of a conference of engineers at Menai Strait discussing how to float one of the tubes of the Britannia Bridge into place.

A contemporary sketch of Robert Stephenson's Britannia Bridge across the Menai Strait.

Arabin Simmons of the Royal Engineers suggested that repeated flexing of the girder weakened it substantially. He found that the main girder had broken in two places, the first break occurring at the centre, while driving a locomotive across the remaining girders showed that they moved by several inches under the load.

Simmons summarised by saying that Robert's design was basically flawed, and that the wrought iron trusses fixed to the girders did not reinforce the girders in any way. The inquest jury reached the same conclusion.

Robert argued that the locomotive derailed while crossing the bridge, and the impact force against the girder caused it to break, but witnesses claimed the girder fractured first. An extra load of ballast that had just been laid over the track as a fire prevention measure may also have contributed to the fracture.

Britannia Bridge today. The structure was severely damaged by a fire on 23 May 1970.

A contemporary sketch of the aftermath of the Dee Bridge disaster.

Following the inquest, a Royal Commission condemned the design and the use of trussed cast iron in railway bridges. The Dee Bridge was later rebuilt using wrought iron.

In 1842, Robert's wife Frances died. They had no children and Robert never remarried.

A right winger, he served as Tory MP for Whitby from 1847 until his death and was a commissioner of the London Metropolitan Commission of Sewers from 1848. He was also president of the Institution of Civil Engineers, for two years from 1855.

Robert died on 12 October 1859 at his London home aged 55, leaving nearly £400,000, and was buried in Westminster Abbey next to Thomas Telford. Queen Victoria granted special permission for his funeral cortege to pass through Hyde Park and spectators bought 3,000 tickets. In his eulogy, he was described as 'the greatest engineer of the present century'.

Robert Stephenson & Company, however, continued to flourish. By the end of the century around 3000 locomotives had been built and a new limited liability company was formed, Robert Stephenson and Company Limited, in 1899. The works relocated to Darlington from where the first locomotive appeared in 1902.

By this time, most British railways were building their own engines, so the company's prime interest had switched to the export market. Many locomotives were supplied for Indian railways, while the firm constructed the first British 2-10-0 for the Argentine Great Western Railway in 1905.

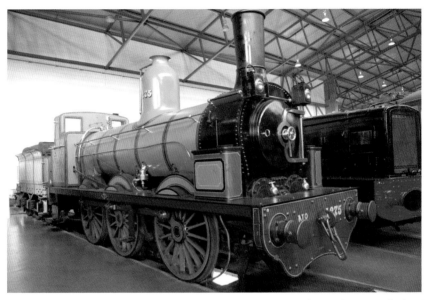

This 0-6-0 built by Dübs & Company in Glasgow is the sole surviving main line tender engine built to Robert Stephenson's 'long boiler' patent of 1833. Supplied in 1874 to the North Eastern Railway, and steamed for the Stockton & Darlington Railway centenary cavalcade in 1925, it is now in the National Railway Museum.

During World War One, the company devoted itself to munitions work and locomotives for the War Department. In the 1920s, 30 2-6-0 mixed traffic locomotives were supplied to the Great Western Railway, 30 0-6-0 tank engines for the London & North Eastern railway and five 2-8-0s for the Somerset & Dorset Joint Railway.

Robert Stephenson & Company locomotive builders' plaque from 1910.

In the mid-thirties, 11 B17 'Sandringham' 4-6-0s were built for the LNER.

Orders had been gradually falling off for the past two decades, and in 1937 the company amalgamated with the locomotive interests of Hawthorn Leslie and Company to form Robert Stephenson & Hawthorns Limited. Main line locomotives were built at Darlington, while Hawthorn Leslie's works at Forth Bank, Newcastle, turned out industrial types. The rights to the Kitson and Manning Wardle companies were acquired in 1938.

Ninety of the famous Hunslet-designed 'Austerity' 0-6-0 saddle tanks were built by the firm for the War Department during World War Two, as well as other saddle tanks for industrial use.

In 1944, a Stephenson wheel turned full circle, when the company was acquired by Vulcan Foundry of Newton-le-Willows, Lancashire. This firm had been founded in 1832 as Charles Tayleur and Company to manufacture girders for bridges, pointwork and crossings, and other ironwork in the wake of the opening of the Liverpool & Manchester Railway, with Robert Stephenson as a partner. Building railway infrastructure components locally made more sense economically than transporting them from Robert's Newcastle works. The Tayleur company became the Vulcan Foundry Company in 1847 and acquired limited liability in 1864.

Locomotives continued to be made: British Railways ordered

Locomotion No 1 taking part in the Stockton & Darlington Railway centenary event in 1925. A similar cavalcade was held at Shildon in 1975 to mark the 150th anniversary. The 50th anniversary of the line's opening was also celebrated in 1875.

eighty GWR-designed 0-6-0 pannier tanks for the Western Region and 35 Class L1 2-6-4Ts for the Eastern Region.

English Electric took over both Vulcan Foundry and Robert Stephenson & Hawthorns in 1955.

The last steam locomotives to be built were an 0-6-0 tank engine in 1958 and a six-coupled fireless locomotive in 1959. The Forth Street works closed in 1960 while the Darlington works switched to building diesel and electric locomotives.

The office block and one workshop of Stephenson's Forth

A medal cast to mark the centenary of the Stockton & Darlington Railway in 1925.

Street Works in South Street, were restored by The Robert Stephenson Trust, before the entire Robert Stephenson & Company and Hawthorn Leslie works sites were bought for redevelopment as the 'Stephenson Quarter'. However, the restored block, along with several associated structures, remain protected by listed building status.

It is impossible to calculate the impact that the Stephensons had not only on the world of railways, but on the world itself. The steam railway provided unprecedented levels of fast efficient transport of both people and freight, opening up continents, creating cities where there had previously been villages, paving the way for the development of the internal combustion engine as manifested in road transport and aircraft, and bringing about the modern world as we know it.

The Stephensons did not invent the steam locomotive or railway, but through *Rocket* steered the concept on course to eventually reach as near to perfection as possible before diesel and electric power took over. Had they never been involved with railways, it is almost certain that other inventors would have filled their places in history, but maybe later than sooner, delaying the progress of transport technology by several years or maybe even a decade or two, as the steam locomotive took longer to perfect. We might also have 5ft 3in gauge main line railways as in Ireland, or Brunel's broad gauge, rather than 4ft 8½in standard gauge.

There is little doubt that without George and Robert, the world would almost certainly look somewhat different today. However, it is the name Stephenson that is indelibly recorded by history.

Maybe the greatest point about this unique father-and-son team is that anyone could 'have a go'. If the son of an illiterate colliery hand who realised the benefits of education could achieve all this, then surely anything is possible if the spirit is willing.

Right: *A George Stephenson memorial plaque inside the National Railway Museum.*

Steam still running on a route George Stephenson built: during the heavy snowfall of December 2010, British Railways Standard 4MT 2-6-0 No 76079 is seen steaming on its home line, the North Yorkshire Moors Railway, which broadly follows the horse-worked Whitby & Pickering Railway.

Picture Credits

Grateful thanks to the following for use of their pictures:

Page 6: National Railway Museum; 9: Ken Brown/Creative Commons; 11: Bill Henderson/Creative Commons; 16: Tyne & Wear Museums; 21: Beamish Museum; 23, top left: Brian Sharpe; 27 top: Parrot of Doom/Creative Commons; 29: Paul Appleton; 45: Philip Benham/North Yorkshire Moors Railway; 48: Crich Tramway Village; 52: Daniel Morgan; 63: Philip Benham/North Yorkshire Moors Railway; 64: Crich Tramway Village.

Stone sleepers from George Stephenson's world's first metre gauge railway at Crich uncovered during developments at Crich Tramway Village.

This 52p stamp depicting George Stephenson was issued by the Royal Mail in 2009 as part of a Pioneers of the Industrial Revolution series.

A commemorative plate made for the Stockton & Darlington Railway 150th anniversary celebrations and now in the National Railway Museum at York.